always know: a book of monk

always know

a book of monk
volumes 1 & 2

john sinclair

assembled @ detroit, may 10, 2020
amsterdam, june 4, 2007 >
november 20, 2008 > january 5, 2014

THE JOHN SINCLAIR FOUNDATION
AMSTERDAM • DETROIT, 2020

Always Know: A Book of Monk
Published by Trembling Pillow Press
New Orleans, LA

ISBN 978-1-7323647-5-2

Cover design and typesetting: Alban Fischer

works by john sinclair

POETRY

This Is Our Music (Artists Workshop Press)
FIRE MUSIC: a record (Artists Workshop Press)
The Poem For Warner Stringfellow (Artists Workshop Press)
Meditations: A Suite For John Coltrane (Artists Workshop Press)
We Just Change The Beat—Selected Poems (Ridgeway Press)
thelonious: a book of monk—volume one (private edition)
fly right—a monk suite (private edition)
Full Circle (minimal press)
Fattening Frogs For Snakes—Delta Sound Suite (Surregional Press)
i mean you—a book for penny (palOmine press)
Song Of Praise: Homage To John Coltrane (Trembling Pillow Press)

WRITINGS

Music & Politics with Robert Levin (Jazz & Pop/World Publishing)
Guitar Army—Street Writings/Prison Writings (Douglas Books)
PeyoteMind (The End Is Near Press)
Va Tutto Bene (en Itaiano) (Stampa Alternativa)
Guitar Army (en Itaiano) (Stampa Alternativa)
Guitar Army (2nd Edition) (Feral House/Process Books)
Guitar Army (en Francais) (Rivage Rouge)
It's All Good—A John Sinclair Reader (Headpress)
Sun Ra Interviews & Essays (Headpress)
It's All Good: A John Sinclair Reader (U.S. Edition—Horner Books)

RECORDINGS

We Just Change The Beat (M/S/A Cassette)
fly right: a monk suite with ed moss (unissued)
thelonious: a book of monk—volume one (New Alliance Records)
Full Moon Night (Alive/Total Energy Records)

If I Could Be With You (Schoolkids Records)

Full Circle with Wayne Kramer (Alive Records)

Underground Issues (SpyBoy Records)

White Buffalo Prayer (SpyBoy Records)

Steady Rollin' Man (triPup Records)

Fattening Frogs For Snakes, Vol. 1—The Delta Sound (Rooster Blues)

Knockout (D-Men Records)

PeyoteMind (The End Is Near Records)

criss cross (Big Chief Records)

Fattening Frogs For Snakes, Vol. 2—Country Blues (No Cover Records)

Fattening Frogs For Snakes, Vol. 3—Don't Start Me To Talking
    (Hill Country Blues)

Tearing Down The Shrine Of Truth & Beauty (LocoGnosis Records)

Detroit Life (No Cover Records)

Viper Madness (No Cover Records)

Let's Go Get 'Em (MoSound Records)

Honoring The Local Gods (Straw2Gold Records)

Song Of Praise: Homage To John Coltrane (Trembling Pillow Press)

Beatnik Youth (Track Records)

Conspiracy Theory (Big Chief Records)

Viperism (Big Chief Records)

Mohawk (IronMan Records)

Keeping The Blues Alive (World Wide Vibe Records)

Beatnik Youth Ambient (IronMan Records)

Mobile Homeland (Funky D Records/Jett Plastic Recordings)

You Buy We Fry—Still Kickin' (Funky D Records)

Fattening Frogs For Snakes Box Set—Volumes 1, 2, 3 & 4 (Jett Plastic
    Recordings)

Digital downloads of all available albums may be ordered from CD Baby

introduction

This suite of poems by John Sinclair is just what the marriage of verse and jazz should be—good on the page, good in the ear, and good in the mind.

Sinclair has undertaken what he calls "an epic investigation in verse of the music, life, times and impact of Thelonious Monk." Starting in 1982, the year Monk passed away, Sinclair has listened carefully to the Monk oeuvre, a series of singles and LPs spanning 1947 to 1972, as it was committed to record, and is writing a poem based on and titled after each recording.

While writing each poem, he listened to the particular Monk cut over and over. To date he has completed more than half of the poems in. four volumes of *always know: a book of monk*, each titled after one period in monk's recording career: "blue notes," "prestige," "riversides" and "columbias."

Many of these extraordinary poems trace moments and movements in the history of modern jazz—poems such as "fly right," "bloomdido," "round about midnight." "monk's mood," "an oscar for treadwell," and "in walked bud." Sinclair is onto an important method of "transmission of mind," tracks that combine the oral tradition of the bard as historian with the brilliant concept of jazz/poetry. It's a form of Investigative Poetry—poetry that tells the stories that stay stories, that could be used in many fields to hand on traditions and beautiful moments.

These poems are a big work that places Sinclair on the path of Olson and other bards who have undertaken long sequences that include personal history as well as the history of a culture and civilization.

In performance, often accompanied by music, The powerful voice of the poet, trembling with the excitement of the music and the stories, plus his phrasing and his respect for his own line breaks, combine to give the tracks an historic energy.

These poems and performances STAY in the head. It's the way poetry and music should be.

This is an extraordinary work

—EDWARD SANDERS

1991 > 2020

contents

VOLUME TWO: PRESTIGE

"all ways know:
   always night,
      all ways know—

& dig the way
   i say
      'all ways'"

—*thelonious monk*

volume one: blue notes

"fly right"

(1917–1947)

for jack kerouac,
who was there

a straight line
drawn across the years
of artistic growth is not

"as the crow flies"
but a nexus
of development, so far

as it goes
there is no strait line
but the accretion of experience

& the many twists &
turns one takes
to gain & measure the sizes

& shapes of activity
& its transformation
into song or verse,

the flight thru geography
& human, material, flesh
& circumstance

to bring a charlie parker
from kansas city to chicago,
new york,

dan wall's chili house,
minton's playhouse in harlem,
a gig in a taxi dance hall

downtown, the particularities
of experience, to be in one place
at one & the same time

out of cheraw, south carolina
to philadelphia, pa.
like a john birks gillespie

who said, if you don't know
why they call me 'dizzy,' you
don't know me very well,

from philly to new york
& the teddy hill orchestra
& cab calloway & duke

& such other aggregations
as would have him
for a week or a month,

the constant fellowship of musicians
riding on buses
through the long american nights,

talking, gambling, eating together
& the burning inside
to make a change in the music,

to enlarge it
so that it would encompass
their enormity of intelligence,

the recognition
& joy, the great leap of the heart
to encounter another

spirit presence
in the same mold, & of i-
dentical shape, from

rocky mount, north carolina
to new york city & back
out on the road

with a faith healer
in a medicine show,
playing for the shake dancers

& pitchmen
& snake oil sellers
all across the south

& the midwest, a gig
with cootie williams & his orchestra
at the savoy ballroom,

the choice of kenny clarke & joe guy
for the house band after
hours at minton's playhouse

in harlem, where monk would meet bird
& dizzy
& charlie christian

& the rest of the cats
& play past dawn, until their music
established itself

& they were the pick
of the greatest of the bandleaders,
earl 'fatha' hines, billy

eckstine, & in monk's
case the father
of the tenor saxophone,

coleman hawkins
& a first recording
for victor, october 19,

1944, before hawk
cut "i mean you"
2 years later, & monk

& charlie parker
& dizzy gillespie
put it all together,

click,
on the stage
of the spotlite club

in the summer of 1946,
the magnificent dizzy gillespie orchestra
with arrangements by tadd dameron & gil fuller—

let us now hail the author
of the "52nd street theme,"
the pace-setter for the modern sound,

a singular individual,
a giant among giants,
a man of whom it can be said

there has never been another
even remotely to resemble him,
a twister & shaper of rhythm & rhyme

& a maker of musical works
which have bent & altered the course
of modern life,

o thelonious, we salute you
at the outset of your career,
we are eager to receive your magic

as it flows into the grooves
of master recording discs of 1947,
we would have your songs & improvisations

re-structure the insides
of our heads
& our hearts, to see out

thru the eyes
which have seen
what you have seen

& to hear
thru the ears
which have no peers—

o monk, if you please!
now grace us
with your incredible music

—detroit institute of arts,
july 7 / greektown,
july 9 & 30, 1985

cincinnati, march 17
& detroit, march 22, 1991
(edit for ed moss & ron esposito)

"thelonious"

for alfred lion & frank wolff

on the 15th
of october,
1947,
5 days following
his 30th birthday,

thelonious sphere monk
was blessed
with his first recording session
as a leader
on blue note records—

the genius
of modern music,
prophet of bebop,
progenitor
of modern jazz,

born in rocky mount,
north carolina, & bred
in "the jungles," west
63rd street,
new york city,

where the piano players
were kings,
& james p. johnson,
willie "the lion" smith,
& numerous of others

populated the neighborhood
both night & day,
before blacks
took over harlem
& moved even further north, this

was the place
where the music was
in new york city,
just a few square blocks
off to the side,

dense
with negroes
from the east coast
& the south,
not mississippi

but atlanta,
charlestown, savannah,
the piney woods
& tobacco country
& virginia,

60 years
after slavery
was abolished,
300 years
after jamestown

unloaded slaves
shipped from west africa,
strangers
in a strange
land,

thelonious monk
was brought to manhattan
as an infant
& began his piano lessons
at age 4,

1921,
surrounded by genius
& the beautifully evolved culture
of africans
in america

—*detroit*
april 1984

"humphf"

for big red

they say monk
couldn't play the music. they say,
monk, he limited
by his own vision

& just can't play right. monk,
he too weird. his music
don't sound right, and he gets up
& dances

while he's playing,
like a jackleg preacher
at a revival meeting
in an old tent in north carolina.

they say monk sound too much
like a whorehouse piano player
from some pre-harlem ghetto
stuffed with back-woods renegades

& sporting women & gamblers,
street-level intellectuals. they say
monk, what is that shit
you trying to play, you just can't

do it that way,
you too way out baby,
that stuff ain't you. & monk
in his infinite knowledge

& wisdom, shoots a grin
from behind the piano,
wiggles his ass on the stool,
lays down another few bars

of utter genius,
turns it over to the tenor player
& rises to dance beside the piano,
some more of that old north carolina boogaloo

—oak park, mi
may 30, 1984

#3

"suburban eyes"

for mary

they say the grass is
always greener
on the other side of the street

but when you get there
it's not, it just
looked like that

for a minute there,
& then it's gone. you're in
the same old place, only the people

are changed,
& the surroundings,
& the quality of life

which is not there. only you
are the same, everything else
is completely different.

now you are not there,
no, now you are the thing
that has changed

or has not changed
in all the confusion. you carry
all the places you've been

around inside of you,
the virginia countryside,
the streets of paterson, new jersey,

the apartments on the east side
of detroit, the northwest side,
in oak park. & now the house

where you brought me
to be all the men in your life,
absent like your father,

present like your two husbands,
or like the uncles who mis-
used you as a child

just like that, there were too
many of them & only the one
of me at hand. so,

although
i was there to stay
you sent me away

& as fate would have it,
the woman i left for you
was good enough to take me back

into the city
& into her heart again
where i intend to remain

      (this is not,
      by the way,
      a monk piece. monk

never left
the middle
of the city

until his work was over
& consequently
the city

never left monk.
& for me, well,
i should have stayed there

in the heart
of the city
where i sure enough belong

—oak park, mi
may 30, 1984/
amsterdam
january 6, 2013

#4

"evonce"

for johnny metcalfe

this is not a monk tune either,
but he probably named it—

like, *evonce*, baby,
you dig?

—*oak park, mi*
may 30, 1984

"nice work if you can get it"

for ken kelley

so begins the second
of monk's 3 sessions
in october & november 1947,

a sly nod
toward his unemployed friends
& a small

tip of the monkian hat
to mr. alfred lion
of blue note records,

busy stockpiling masters
against the recording ban
of 1948, & possessed

of enough good taste
& intelligence
to bring in monk,

gene ramey & art blakey
to cut these musical gems
& leave them to shine

for our enrichment
& delight
as long as there are records

—*detroit*
march 16, 1985

#6

"ruby, my dear"

for estelle

a red candle
burning in a red
glass on a red tablecloth
in a dark corner

of a darkened nightclub,
a cigarette
burning in a red
plastic ashtray, a chesterfield

king
with lipstick red
on the end
& the smoke

from the cigarette in her eyes,
her hair is black satin
against skin of chocolate brown
or golden cream, or any of the million

gorgeous hues of american women
of african descent, purest black
to highest yellow
& every imaginable shade

in between, this is a song
to the woman in the red dress,
erzulie, or ruby
my dear

as monk would have her
pinned against the keyboard,
lush in the hips & thighs,
lush of lips & breasts,

the most beautiful ass
in the history of western civilization,
turned out over the top
of the thighs, out

to the western edge of africa
& back to the states again
to meet the small of her back,
the smell of jasmine & musk

rising from her flesh
in the closeness & warmth
of the tiny room, her eyes
so impossibly soulful

trained on the bandstand,
the band is bird,
monk on piano,
mingus & shadow wilson

at 3:00 am sunday morning,
a bottle of champagne
half drunk on the table,
the music is soft & sweet

yet as deep with intelligence
& spirit as the woman herself—
"ruby, my dear"
filling her big heart with song

—detroit
january 12, 1985

"well you needn't"

for skip williamson

if there is something
to be learned
from the study of monk's
works (& there is)

there is no reason
to rhyme
nor to add beats
where they need not exist

except as the flow
or the rise & fall
of the composer's heartbeat,
or the pattern it makes

through the pulsation
in the brain, or the beat
of one's blood
through the veins & arteries,

back & forth through the body
or the brain
or the paths that are taken in life
& shape what one sees

or hears or feels
or fails to feel, these
& only these mark the lines
of the work

& give it what form
or course it may take, nothing
but what's there
to be used, no more

& no less, the materials
of song or verse,
"directly from my heart
to yours," & that's that

—*greektown, detroit*
july 30, 1985

#8

"april in paris"

for george tysh

if there are standards
against which
we stand to be measured
or measure ourselves

& are found wanting, like
i want to be in paris
in april
but i'll be in detroit

instead, which is a whole
different place indeed,
or we find we "measure up"
or go so far beyond the mark

like monk on "april
in paris," or bird with strings
or the wild bill davis arrangement
by basie, "let's hear it

one more once," this is not at all
what those squares had in mind
when they wrote this shit
for some corny broadway musical,

junkies shooting dope
& playing they songs in-
side out like that,
turning broadway upside down

& shaking a few pitiful coins
out its pockets,
these are "standards"
because everybody knows them,

little simple melodies
hammered into the public body
thru sheer repetition,
blam blam blam blam blam,

20 or 30 times a day,
always the same fucking way,
little pop tunes with a bare modicum
of invention & intelligence

except as they are invested
& propelled beyond their premises
by the genius of a monk
or a bird or bud powell,

giants of spontaneous composition,
total masters of creative abstraction,
turning the western world
on its ear,

april in paris
or autumn in new york,
they set a standard so high
we are still trying to reach it

—detroit
june 1984 >
january 12 , 1985

#9

"off minor"

("what now")

for nkenge zola

monk's birth certificate
calls him 'thelius'
& puts him here on earth
in 1917. some time later

monk enters our lives
as thelonious sphere monk
with 3 years lopped
off his age. the symmetry

must have been irresistible
to the young master
of rhythm & rhyme—
10, 10, 20, or

1 & 1 is 2
with those 3 round zeros
marching across the page
off minor like that

—*oak park, mi*
may 30, 1984

"introspection"

("playhouse")

for bob "righteous" rudnick

i remind my mother
of all the men
she couldn't stand:

the unknown man
who molested her
as a girl—

her brother lyle,
the playboy ex-
gangster ex-con—

my father jack
who left her at 60
for a younger woman—

but it's exactly
the same way
for me:

everything i hate in women
always reminds me
of my mother

—kalamazoo, mi
december 6, 1984

#11

"in walked bud"

for les reid & john petrie

first there was monk
before the war
& then from further up-
town, in harlem,

from the neighborhood
of coleman hawkins, sonny
rollins, & jackie mclean,
there was bud powell

or earl alfred "bud" powell
on piano, strict interpreter
of dizzy & bird
for the keyboard, fleet

of single line & fast
to abandon
the heaviness in the left hand,
to make room for the bass & drums

& the harmonic
implications
of the melody, the farther
reaches

of the chords, the dizzy
atmosphere
which resulted
from the compression of experience

& the deep urban intelligence
eof african-americans
born in manhattan
or brought to harlem as children,

coming up on the streets,
standing outside of bars
& after-hours joints with the whores
& the dope peddlers, straining

to listen
or to hear from the bandstand
or to see the musicians inside
with such aspirations, to get up there

themselves, with they little horns,
behind the drums, or at the piano,
hands on the keyboard
& a room full of people

looking up
from the depths of their lives
to flood the bandstand
with huge waves of love

& warmth, then back out
to the streets, & the ugly
stares, the cold
bitter hatred

of the white people,
the nightstick
across the head
in philadelphia, the loss

of consistent memory,
the shock treatments
inside the several nut houses,
a phony dope beef in new york city

& no more cabaret card,
loss of license to work
in the nightclubs of manhattan
or even brooklyn, iced

out
of everything
but the will to make music
out of the guts of a piano,

the amazing bud powell,
the blazing bud powell,
now faltering
& lost, now lucid, now

gone
again, in toronto
with bird & dizzy
& mingus & max roach,

fresh out of creedmore
& more shocks to the head,
may, 1953, on the same night
rocky marciano

knocked out jersey joe wolcott,
drunk & crazy bud powell
back in manhattan, a night
at birdland with bird

in the first week of march,
1955, gone all the way out
of his motherfucking mind,
bud powell,

bud powell,
bud powell,
bird's voice ringing in his ears,
mingus pointing his finger

from the bandstand,
"these are sick men,"
he said, "ladies &
gentlemen, please

don't associate me
with this madness," & in
walked monk that night
to catch some music, with his head

set straight on his shoulders
& his feet
firmly on the ground, in control
of his faculties

like few men of any time,
1955, just a week before bird
would leave us here
& bud would stagger on,

the scene changes,
time waits,
exile in paris
from 1959 to the end

of his life, but on this night
at birdland there they are,
bird at the microphone
intoning his name & bud

staring off into space, & monk
taking it all in,
crazy
too, like a fox

to say to bird & bud, "i
told you guys
to act crazy, but i
didn't

tell you
to fall in love
with the act. you're *really*
crazy now. . . ."

—*louisville , ky october 12 , 1985/*
detroit
december 7–14 , 1985

#12

"monk's mood"

("why do you evade the facts?")

for melba boyd & sadiq muhammad

what would piss you off
if you were monk
but the superficial gesture,

the appropriation
of the formal
weirdness

without the content
or any intent
to keep the code

of manly conduct, that what one says
& what one does must be one
& the same

or either bullshit reigns
& walks & talks
like a man, but no man

is there to be found
in the action, like hats & beards
& funny names, or dreadlocks

& canes, the constant iteration
of the sainted litany
of the great masters

as a form
of intimidation—the pointed
finger, the crooked

tongue, the phony shit
that monk despised
& not the word made act, no pose

but for real,
no crooked intention
or weird overlay, like

this cat is a chump,
let's set him up, we can
get the money out the bank

without him knowing about it
& not pay the other musicians
for the concert

& blame it on him,
that they never got paid
& put some crow jim

shit in the game too,
like it's about color
or anything else but sincerity

of expression, depth
of soul,
intelligence, it's not about

race it's about
culture,
motherfucker,

like what you learn
from constant exposure
to what people be doing,

it is learned or ac-
quired, from birth on
or from when you be born into it,

like the way the music
can be studied, & the life
& the code of behavior can get in

to the sound, like monk & james
p. johnson,
willie "the lion" smith,

the cats in his neighborhood
& in harlem
where monk was well known

the piano players
hung out together,
they bought each other drinks

& meals,
or a place to stay,
but they took care of each other

with no hand
in the other cat's pocket, no
knife in the back,

no phony shuck &
jive, twisted, super
hip sneer on they jibs,

straight-ahead cats
with the ethics
that made them for real

men of music
we worship & study
long after they have passed from this sphere

—detroit / august 1 > september 15 > december 18 23, 1985 ·
july 7, 1989

edit for steve gebhardt
wvxu-fm, cincinnati
may 14, 1991

"who knows"

for marion brown

"everything i play
is different,"
monk said—

"different melody,
different harmony,
different structure. each piece

is different
from the other one.
i have a standard,

& when the song
tells a story, when it
gets a certain

sound,
then it's through
. . . completed."

& steve lacy adds, monk
"told me
he never does anything

unless he wants to do it,
& he's the only man i've ever met
who really does do

exactly what he want to
with no jive at all, just exactly
what he wants to do." & finally,

for the 3rd thing,
monk says "when i
was a kid, i felt something

had to be done
about all that jazz. so
i've been doing it

for 20 years. maybe i've turned
jazz
another way. maybe

i'm a major
influence. i don't know. anyway,
my music

is *my* music,
on my piano,
too. that's a criterion

of something. jazz
is my adventure. i'm after new chords,
new ways of syncopating,

new figurations,
new runs. how to use notes
differently. that's it,

just how
to use notes
differently"

—detroit
november 10, 1985

reference: joe goldberg,
jazz masters of the 50's

"round about midnight"

for linda jones

there is a point
between night & day
where it all comes clear
& bright, a new beginning

where yesterday
can be left behind
& a new day is there
to greet us, clean

with promise
& a clear path
thru the hours before dawn
when the mind kicks in,

the squares all tucked in bed
& the people of the night
in charge of the scene—players,
musicians, whores,

countermen at diners & cats
delivering the morning papers,
garbagemen & cops & drunks
in the rhythms of midnight

& the small hours after,
a different sphere completely
from daytime, traffic
& the peculiar world of commerce—

this is when the music is made,
in nightclubs until 2
or 4 a.m., & then in after-
hours joints & people's cribs,

or in the recording studios
after the gig, with everyone nice
& relaxed, half-
juiced or hazy,

lazy, a little crazy maybe
but ready to put down some tunes
onto recording discs or tape
for the rest of the world to hear—

round midnight & after, the end
of a day, or in the meta-
phorical mode, it's the last sigh
of an era, like around 1939

thru '44, with the war
going on abroad, & the nation
finally tearing itself loose
from the last dying grip

of pre-modern america,
all its young men at war
& only the rejects, mis-
fits & draft-dodgers left

to shape some new form
from the ruins of the past,
some measure of their alienation
from the day before,

their allegiance to the flag
of tomorrow, like whatever
it might bring would be better
than what's happening right now,

the high discovery
of risk, or the existential premise
that something new & brilliant can be made
from the existing materials,

the intention
"to create & invent
on little jobs" that monk
spoke of in 1948, with no reward

but the beauty of the thing itself,
the challenge of invention
with no idea of what might come next,
no pattern to fall back on,

nothing but the driving force in-
side your self, & the long roots of culture
stretching back to west africa
& the southern united states,

the utter & absolute beauty
of making a bridge
across the years, to link the past
in a whole new way

with what would come next,
round about midnight
of a dying world, & round about
3 a.m. of a brand new day,

monk at the piano
composing the future
& bud powell taking the piece
to cootie williams to record,

1944, a standard of modern music
even before its composer could record it,
the loveliest work in modern jazz
at just over 3 minutes long

yet longer than tomorrow,
longer than the 45 years
since monk eased it out of his head
& his gargantuan heart

& gave it to us,
"round about midnight," as a sign
that something was coming
that had never been here before

—detroit
july 14 > december 27–30, 1985

"all the things you are"

for kenny "pancho" hagood

on this bright day
in 1948, as the sun
set over manhattan

& the recording ban
continued to eclipse the music
of one of the most fertile years

in the history of afro-america,
alfred lion took monk
& my man kenny "pancho" hagood

& milt jackson,
both out of the dizzy gillespie orchestra
& the west side of detroit,

& john simmons & shadow
wilson, for rhythm
into harry smith's apex studios

for an outlaw date, to begin with
another slap in the face
of the corpse of jerome kern

whose widow had barred the release
of dizzy's magnificent works
incorporating the lightweight themes of kern—

mrs. k contended her
hubby's legacy had been defiled
by the glorious improvising of diz

on his tunes, which had after all been written
for some ridiculous oscar
hammerstein entertainment—so monk

& bags & pancho, in an in-
effable mood, stretched out jerome's bones
over an open fire

& toasted the dead tunesmith
once more over easy
& left him for the dogs of time

to chew up
& spit out
at their infinite leisure

—maximus & co.
birmingham, mi
july 2, 1985

#16

"i should care"

for kenny "pancho" hagood

"bird
never excited me

like he did
the others,"

says monk. "'bird
is a god,' they said.

"he wasn't to me! no,
& no one

else was,
either!"

—*detroit*
november 10, 1985

reference: joe goldberg
jazz masters of the 50's, *p. 31*

#17

"evidence"

for penny

if it were just
you, just me,
or as monk would
have it,

justice
would be served
but our sentence
is not so short

& our court-
ship's been so long—oh,
if it were just
the 2 of us, to start

a new life
together, but let the record
indicate,
the evidence

is piled up
all over town—
my older daughter
living here with me,

my younger
with her mother,
your older daughter
over with your mother

& the little one
holed up with you—
a chord
structure under-

pinning whatever melody
or song we can make of it—
not just us, baby, but the fine
fine thing fate has made of us

—detroit
june 24, 1982

#18

"mysterioso"

for rick steiger

not quite so mysterious
but oh so, mister, so
strange & manly, like monk

could make it sound,
going up & down the scale
with such deliber-

ation, like he had all
the time in the world
to delineate his meaning, in life too

he may have seemed
strange & mysterious
as he walked the sidewalks

of west 63rd street, hat
& beard to limn his image,
shades with bamboo frames

were so very hip, yes, but oh so
functional, perhaps, to cover
the cast in his eye—

a popular figure, monk,
they say, at home
in his skin & at one

with the people
around him, the kids
especially

around the neighborhood
would greet him
with some glee, a family

man & raconteur, monk
went home at night
to nellie, or stayed in

for years at a time
if he felt like it, or moved
over to jersey with the baroness

& barry harris, he kept
his own clock
exactly as he felt it, went

where he wanted to go & saw
what he wanted
to see, mister

ra or mister ree,
to you or to me,
whoever he wanted to be

—detroit
july 3 > december 7, 1985 >
july 7, 1989

#19

"epistrophy"

for roy brooks

there is no such world
as that which exists
in books, or such con-

tractions & expansions
as we may devise
for ourselves,

out of the endless chaos
of real life, nothing
is so ordered

as we would make it,
mere trophies
of epistemology

brought back from the battle
to make sense out of something
which makes no sense

whatsoever
except what registration
of feeling & experience

we can make in song
& keep singing it like monk
all life long

—new orleans
march 4, 1984/
detroit
may 24, 1984

52

#20

"i mean you"

for penny

it's not just a case
of wanting to be in love

as if it didn't matter
just who you are

or the particularities, like
the way you make my blood race,

the certain taste of your skin,
or just how soulful you are

in every way, & how deeply
& completely you understand me

in all the nutty complexity
of my being—it's your intelligence,

your exquisite taste in music,
& the warmth of you i want,

baby, the warmth of *you* i want
like i've never wanted anyone else

—detroit
september 18, 1984

#21

"bloomdido"

for amiri baraka

in the beginning
of the modern
era,

in harlem,
in the early days
of the new

music,
in the days of war
when bird

& diz & monk
made it all
start

to happen, in
harlem
late at night

the music hit
hard
& deep, monk

& bird & dizzy
turned it all around
& made it

fit
what was happening
in new york city,

the war,
the sound of modern
city

life, in harlem
or in midtown,
downtown,

monk & bird
& dizzy
made the music fit,

they made it
fit, they
made

the music
come to life,
they made life

come to the music,
they made it
bloom—

bloomdido,
bloomdido,
bloom ditty bop

bop bop,
they made it bloom
like a gigantic flower

or millions of flowers
in a magnificent garden,
bop,

they gave it life
& made it bloom,
dido,

bop,
& great flowers emerged
in the middle of the night,

they made it bloom,
they gave it life,
they made it all happen at once

—*traverse city, michigan*
august 24, 1985/
athens, ohio
march 1, 1986

#22

"an oscar for treadwell"

for paul lichter, ron esposito
& the great oscar treadwell

shoot a straight line
back thru time, from the 6th of june
1950, midway
thru the 20th century—

shoot it thru the centerpoint
of a human triangle
made of spirit & flesh,
monk & bird & dizzy—

shoot it back to the end
of the 1930's
in new york city,
harlem, clark monroe's

uptown house
at 132nd st. & 7th ave,
on the old site of the rhythm club,
where the set started at 4 am

& the house band was bird sometimes,
vic coulson & george treadwell on trumpets,
allen tinney piano, ebenezer paul
on bass, & from brooklyn

a very young max roach
at the drums—& leading the band,
the man with the plan so tight
that they named the joint after him,

clark monroe,
"the dark gable,"
with a sharp eye for business
& a regular hit for the band

in midtown, every night
from 9 pm to 3 am,
seven days a week
with every seventh week off—

georgie jay's 78th st. taproom
employed this splendid ensemble
with clark monroe doing his little dance steps
fronting the band all night

& then they would tear off
to harlem & hit
after the taproom gig
from 4 to 8 am

at the uptown house
7 mornings a week, all juiced up
& ready to cook thru dawn
with anybody who was ready to sit in—

the clark monroe outfit
set the pace
with its tight little arrangements
& the trumpet of vic coulson

& players would come up to monroe's
from all over town,
after their gigs,
or if they were in the city

with the big bands that toured
they would come up to harlem
& get with what was happening
in the jazz center of the world,

where the cats who could really play
were cutting a new edge
on the shape of the music, pointing it
into the future, out in

front of them, where they could kick it
square in the ass
& make it go
where it had never gone

before—in 1942
when the new music
called bebop was new, like even before
it was called bebop, & monk

& bird & dizzy
were wild young men of music
with insane ideas
& incredible technique,

desperate
to push the music
forward—
at clark monroe's uptown house

where coleman hawkins & roy eldridge,
say, & 5 cats from the glenn
miller band, plus lester young,
billie holiday,

a few students from columbia
including jack kerouac
& jerry newman, who took down the music
on his little wire recorder

that his daddy bought him for college,
plus some sailors on leave,
whores, pimps, & dope sellers,
young musicians like monk

& benny harris, there might be
dexter gordon in town from the west coast
with the benny carter orchestra
& more cats from harlem

with their lady friends,
this would be the crowd
between 4 and 8 in the morning
when the music would start to take off

& bird would play some shit on "cherokee"
that would make people's jaws drop,
whew,
where did *this* motherfucker come from,

thrusting his intelligence & drive
into the heart
of the old music, cutting a new channel
where something could be said

about what was happening right now,
bam,
bop,
splee dooley ooo bop,

this was the way so many people
had been feeling inside, & say dizzy
climbs up on the stand
& puts in his 200 million dollars' worth

& suddenly there is monk
at the piano, & kenny clarke
'klook mop' on drums,
& coleman hawkins says whoah, let me

get up there with these young bloods
& feel this out for myself,
ba-weep,
spla-doop,

sploo-eee doolee ree-bop,
this is the *shit,*
blooo-wee bop she bam,
the heavens opened up & the holy feeling

entered the participants
from above & below, until they were infused
with the new spirit
of the new music,

blue-eee bop,
beee-eee-eee-bop,
bird & monk & dizzy
wailing thru the harlem night

at clark monroe's uptown house,
turning on the world
& spinning it around
on a whole different axis

—kansas city, mo
november 14, 1986/
detroit,
may 27 > july 22 > september 28, 1987

#23

"mohawk"

for rev. goat carson

let us not read too much
into the titles of this session,
june 6, 1950,
bird & dizzy & monk

with curley russell on bass
& buddy rich so out of
place on drums, if max roach
had been on hand

to make this band hit
with a different edge
on the music, but that's jazz
& the way it has to play

with the specific individuals
who be on the set
that night, the music
of the men on the stand

& what we call it
just does not matter,
bird told symphony sid
in a radio interview

concerning these sessions, like he had
no idea how these songs
had got their names, he said
"it's all just

gone
music, man" and "i just
call them 'rhythm'
or 'blues' & they put

the names on them
after i've left the studio." monk,
on the other hand,
composed his music

on his own progressions
& fit the songs
to the names he gave them,
such precision

of rhythm & rhyme
as we see so rarely,
to take the hair off
the sides of the head

& leave just a strip
along the top,
scalping all pretense
for the baldness of statement,

building a new music
on the bones of the old
like bird, or like monk
with a whole new structure

of sound, breathing life
of its own, like nothing
that had ever
existed before—

mohawk, mo-
hawk, monk & bird
& dizzy
creating a nation of music

& chopping away
at the dead flesh
& hair & muscle & bone
of what had been left for them

—athens, ohio
march 1, 1986/
new york city
april 3, 1986

#24

"my melancholy baby"

for stevenson palfi

in the awful aftermath
of hurricane katrina,
amid the wreckage
of his city,

his neighborhood,
his home,
his painstaking work
& his life itself,

looking forward to nothing
but increasing pain
& suffering beyond measure
as far as he could see,

the relentless public indifference
to the fruits of his labors,
the bitter impossibility
of completing his allen toussaint film

already 15 years in the making,
songwriter: unknown,
pieced together in fits
& starts, when he could wheedle

enough bread for a shoot
or get a print made
or edit something together
so he could see it—money

he had to beg for
from people at arts agencies
who couldn't stand him
& tried to ruin his life,

or people who dug his work
but never gave him enough cash
to make it all happen
the way it was supposed to,

this beautiful cat
with a big heart
& huge imagination, & a mind
that never stopped working,

the creator of "piano players
rarely ever play together"
starring professor longhair
& tuts washington

& the great toussaint,
documenter of emmanuel sayles
& papa john creach
& jabbo "junebug" jones,

employer of my daughter celia
& treasured friend & accomplice
ever since that day in 1982
when me & harry duncans

banged on his front door
on banks street
& begged him
to let us see "piano players"

& he showed it to us—
& that's the way i'll re-
member him, a guy who gave
& gave of what he had,

smiling through the pain
that wracked his body
& his heart, in love
with his work

& his daughter nell
& the music we all love—
always & forever,
brother stevenson palfi,

always in love with the music

—st. philip st, new orleans
december 30, 2005 >
february 22, 2006/
rochester, ny
january 19, 2007

"leap frog"

for steve cannon

over the top
of everything
that's come before, & then

hunched down
for the future
to vault over your back,

lest we forget
that these are young men,
playful yet deep

with intelligence, bursting
with the joy of discovery
& their unparalleled virtuosity,

beautifully seasoned
in the history & practice
of their music

& sure enough de-
termined
to move the music forward—

leap frog, leap
frog, bird & monk & dizzy
in the days before the second world war

—north rampart street
new orleans
december 10, 1996

#26

"relaxin' with lee"

for andrew jones, larry hayden & henk botwinik

mr. lee bridges was around
for a very long time
& never a square,
he lived 77 years
& carried himself so humbly
all over the world
in his infinite hipness,

never at a loss
for a way to make it
through whatever troubles
might present themselves
& come out on top
with his dignity intact,
& his splendid wardrobe

& his beautiful smile,
always revealing
the radiant warmth
of his personality & hustling
his little books of poetry
& his memoirs
& his heartfelt performances,

relaxed & at home
wherever he went
with his hundreds of friends
who loved him so madly,
mr. lee bridges
was just about the sweetest man
you would ever want to meet,

from the '40s & '50s
when he followed the music
from detroit to new york city
& all the high points
in between, smoking reefers
with king pleasure & hanging out
with all the cats on the scene,

then making his way
across the ocean
in the early '60s, smuggling hashish
from morocco & the orient
to paris & amsterdam
& reading his poems in the streets
& the coffeeshops & cafes,

mr. lee bridges,
the cannabis poet,
a great American
& an exemplary human being
who graced our lives with love
like no one else on earth
& lives now forever in our hearts

—detroit
april 2005/
rochester, ny
january 18, 2007

#27

"especially to you"

for estelle

dear sugar,
i wanted to tell you
all about the way
you make me feel,

how deeply
you move me, how
warm & happy i feel
when i'm talking with you,

the way you arouse me
even on the telephone,
or looking in your eyes
or watching you walk

across the room, your ass
is so beautiful
it should be on display
at the detroit institute of arts,

city of magnificent booties,
sugar you've got the most gorgeous
behind in town,
if i may say so,

& your pretty little titties
with the big chocolate nipples
that i love to feast my eyes on,
my hands & lips,

& speaking of feasting
i could worship forever
at the sweet shrine of venus
between your incredible legs,

bury my tongue deep
in your delicious pussy,
how good it feels to lick it
& rub it on my face,

i love your thighs
& calves & knees, i
love to suck your toes
or your fingers

squeezing my cock,
& when i get to your mouth
it'll be hard to stop
singing your praises—like your lips

are made the way the god of lips
intended all lips to be,
full & shapely,
irresistable to the touch

of my mouth, or tongue
or dick
nuzzled between your lips,
"harder than chinese arithmetic"

& kissing your mouth itself
is another fantastic thrill,
your tongue on fire
but all wet & alive

under my tongue,
how sweetly you suck
on my lower lip,
& your teeth too—

i'm insane about your teeth,
how they push out
against your upper lip,
the sexy spaces between them,

the way you keep them covered up
until i can make you smile or laugh
& you reveal them to me
& the long corners of your mouth turn up

& your beautiful cheekbones,
high, probably cherokee,
geechee, definitely mississippi,
did i mention the colors

of your skin, deep browns so rich
& your eyes,
with that little sleepy drift
in the left one,

i love to kiss you in your ears
& slide my tongue down
under your jaw,
along your perfect neck,

i love the way you wear your hair,
the way you smell,
your wide african nose,
your wrists & hands,

i even love the stretch marks
& other evidence
of the birth
of four babies,

i think of your wet pussy
so hot & juicy
yet so tight & snug,
unloosened by childbirth—

sugar, if i could make these words
throb & grip my dick
like the sugary walls of your cunt
i'd be the greatest poet on earth—

but let me sing of your charms
in my feeble verse, & dwell
on your spiritual qualities,
the emormous size of your heart,

the love & care you take
with your remarkable children,
your fierce intelligence
& determination to get over,

i love you for who you are
& what you've done with it
& most of all, for the person
that you want to be

& i want to be there with you
in the land of milk & honey,
sweet sugar,
i want to be there with you

when all your dreams come true
& your efforts are rewarded
& i can take you in my arms
& make love to you for ever

with all your worries set to rest
& your troubles gone for good,
just you & me & our big fat smiles
& a rainbow arching across the sky

—*in transit,*
detroit-new orleans,
august 20, 1987/

cafe du monde,
new orleans,
august 24, 1987

"nobody knows (nobody cares)"

this is a song
that's rarely been heard
& a session of which the poet knows
nothing

but for the listings
in the discographies
announcing the presence
of the featured vocalist,

mr. frankie passions,
with whom two cuts were made,
including the previous song
& the prophetically-titled number

which we know here
only by its name,
absent the opportunity to hear
what exactly it sounds like—

what happened to these tracks
lost in the smaze of musical history?
yo, just like the song say,
nobody knows (nobody cares)

—greektown, detroit,
august 27, 1987/
amsterdam
January 6, 2013

#29

"four in one"

for penny

sweetheart, we
've had three
trial sepa-

rations now
& none of them
has worked out

like we thought we
wanted them to—
maybe this time

we'll wise up for once
& stay together
the rest of the way

—kalamazoo, mi
december 6, 1984

#30

"criss cross"

for penny,
on our 15th wedding anniversary

ever since that night
at cobb's corner
in 1979, when I saw you criss-

crossing the floor, your perfect ass a-
swing & a-sway, oh
it was love

at first sight, & I've stayed that way
through all the crazy changes
we managed to endure, criss-

crossing in & out
of each other's lives, splitting up
& coming back together

so many times, until we were joined
as husband & wife at last
on that bright first day of 1989—

& 15 years later, I still love you
more every day, & I'll keep on loving you
as long as I have life

& if I have to be so far a-
way from you
on this lucky day, I'm out here criss-

crossing the ocean to find
a place where I can bring you
to live out our days together, baby,

oh yeah—*happily ever after*

—amsterdam
december 26, 2003/
's-graveland
january 3, 2004/
rotterdam
january 7, 2004

#31

"eronel"

for ken mikolowski & steve the fly

edgar allen poe
played backwards,

like a raven
in a mirror,

or a cask of amontillado
upside down,

a twisted glimpse
into the mind of monk at work

—*oak park, mi*
march 20, 1984/

amsterdam
january 7, 2013

#32

"straight no chaser"

for art blakey

"years ago,"
art blakey recalls,
"i was talking with thelonious
& he said, 'when you

hit the bandstand
the bandstand
is supposed to lift
from the floor

& the people
are supposed to be
lifted up
        too'."

—harmonie park
detroit
june 25, 1988

reference: arthur taylor,
notes and tones: musician to musician interviews
(perigee books, 1982), p. 248

#33

"ask me now"

for joyce

if you thought i was
feeding you a line
when i said i fell

head over heels for you
i want you to know i
couldn't be more

upside down in love, you
irresistable, mmmmm de-
lectable, every day is

so much better with you
in the middle now
of my life

—annunciation st.
new orleans
mardi gras morning
march 6, 1984

#34

"willow weep for me"

for penny

i know a man who loves you
is a hard thing to give up,
but when the good feeling
is gone, & all you can think of
is how bad things had gotten

& the thought of a future
with the same man
even though he loves you
is a terrifying prospect
because you just don't want him

any more, i know you feel
we've been through this thing together
too many times
to make it work
if we try it again—

five times we've been in love
& lived as man & wife,
five times we've split apart,
five years since we married,
three months since we've been apart—

now i have to learn to live
without you in my life
though it's not what i would choose—
i'm the man who loves you,
baby, but you don't want me no more

—*superior street*
detroit
july 26, 1993

#35

"skippy"

for dr. dorothy

to skip out
with no word
of warning, & abandon
the foreseeable future

without reason
or thought of tomorrow
or the days to come,
& wipe out

our long year together
with no care
for what might come next—
then like they used to say,

if you think
that shit will work
then, baby, skippy
is a goddamned sissy

—fossa cesia >
roma, italy
june 30 > july 1, 2007

#36

"hornin' in"

for penny

okay, so i saw other women
when i was out on the road
in '86 & '87, just like
you always suspected,

& then they would call you
to say terrible things
over the phone
while i was in some other city,

that crazy lady from k.c.,
a woman friend in chicago,
but you never heard from niambi
in new york city, or sweet margarita

down in new orleans—
yes, i saw these ladies
as much as i could, & only wished
there were more of them

at the time, out on the road
with a 7-piece band
working $300 gigs in college bars
& staying in cheap motels

from st. petersburg to stowe,
vermont, & all through the midwest
with the bills piling up at home
& no way to pay them,

your jaws would be so tight
when I'd get back to detroit
you might not even kiss me
for three or four days

or you'd send me off on another trip
with my nerves all tied up
& screaming, like you didn't even care
what i was going through

& you had it right again,
i never should've went out there
& left you behind, trying to feed
three or four teenage girls

with no money to work with
& no help from me, it's no wonder
you felt so bad, but i never cared,
it was all your fault to me

& i never looked back
until it was too late
& you had horned me out
where i belonged,

the band broke up,
the road was ended,
you put me out & no
other women

could replace you
as much as i might try, no one else
could make my life en-
tire again, until i could start to see

just how wrong i had been
& picked up the phone at last
to horn back in on you again
baby, hornin' in on you

—*harmonie park, detroit
march 21 > may 27, 1988 >
october 31, 1988 >
august 10, 1990*

"sixteen"

("unorthodoxy")

for penny

i've been in love with you
for 16 years, since the night
i first spotted you
across the room at cobb's corner

& through all the ups
& downs our course
has laid for us, two headstrong lovers
determined to get what we want

from each other & from
the world at large, un-
orthodox to the bone
but just as much in love with each other

as any two people can be—
baby, now it's 7 years
since our wedding day, & i'm more crazy
about you than ever before

—french quarter
new orleans
december 22, 1995
for our 7th anniversary

#38

"carolina moon"

for thelonious monk

just so each day
dawns again
& everything is new
all over—

were it not for you,
o great monk,
& your magic
ilk, it would

stay the same way
all the time, that
big fat stinky moon
just rotting in the sky

—renaissance center bus stop,
detroit
september 27, 1982

#39

"let's cool one"

for joyce

in the words
of the perpetual romantic,
if love ain't everything

then it just ain't love
& if it can't be
as hot as all that,

let's cool one
for a minute & see
just how hot it can be

& if the fire's still there
like the bard once put it,
you'll be the first to know

—oak park
may 30, 1984/
amsterdam
June 4, 2007

#40

"i'll follow you"

for penny

i've spent more
than a quarter of a century
with you em-
bedded at the center

of my life, & i'm still
just as crazy about you
as i've always been,
even though

you may never join me
in the life i'm seeking
on the other side
of the atlantic ocean,

but now
i'm right here
in the motor city
& you don't want to see me,

i guess i thought
you would never leave me be-
hind, but how wrong
can a motherfucker be,

& now it would seem
that you've started a
new life for yourself
without me in it,

& i wouldn't blame you,
to find another man
who can be there for you
when you need him, & help you

with your troubles,
& hold you
through the cold detroit nights
& bring you

whatever semblance of happiness
you are able to secure—oh,
if i've lost you
i've lost the love

of my life, heart
of my heart, lover
of my wildest dreams,
forgiver of my trespasses,

faithful companion
& partner in crime
as long as you could see fit,
you've followed me so long

against all possible odds
& i can feel you turning a-
way from me
although not a word

has been spoken
but if you don't want me
i won't stand in your way,
if i can't make it right

& there's no happy ending
to our protracted romance
I'll step out of your life
& wish you the best,

my baby,
all the best of everything
i wish i could give you
for the rest of your life

—detroit
august 20 > 30–31, 2005/
amsterdam
october 10, 2005/
rochester ny
january 18, 2007

volume two: prestige

"little rootie tootie"

for my brother david

my little brother
died in his sleep last night
at the age of 63—

david albert sinclair,
born in flint, michigan
may 31, 1945

passed away
in defuniak springs, florida
october 22, 2008—

a beautiful cat
from beginning to end,
poet & music lover,

12-year-old drummer
with tommy lattner
& the tom cats,

all star basketball
& football player
at davison high school,

president of his class,
brilliant student
& accomplished scholar,

off to dartmouth college
on a football scholarship
in the fall of 1963,

switched to poetry
& staged little readings
in a laundromat off of campus,

completed his studies somehow
& came to detroit
in the spring of 1967

to make the artists workshop
an even better place
with his selfless energy

& iron commitment
to the life of poetry,
music & social change

we had come to embrace
& make real
in our own lives—

oh my brother david,
my beautiful little brother
for 63 years,

editor of *work* magazine,
manager of the rock & roll band
called the up,

principal & backbone
of trans-love productions
& the trans-love energies commune,

chief of staff
of the white panther party
& the rainbow people's party

& the defense team
for the cia conspiracy trial
in which i was a defendant,

who carried the entire load
for his big brother
while i was in prison,

spearhead
of the free john sinclair campaign
for 2-1/2 years,

producer
with peter andrews
of the john sinclair freedom rally

with john lennon & yoko ono,
stevie wonder,
bobby seale,

allen ginsberg,
ed sanders,
phil ochs,

archie shepp & roswell rudd,
cjq,
commander cody

& his lost planet airmen,
bob seger
with teegardin & van winkle,

the up,
bob rudnick,
jerry rubin & all the rest

with a cast of thousands
smoking marijuana by the pound
on the floor of crisler arena

& the vast public outcry
prompted by the concert
that got me out of prison

3 days later,
hallelujah,
to return to ann arbor

to work with my brother
& leni sinclair
& my comrades in the party,

gary grimshaw,
frank bach & peggy taube,
pun & genie plamondon,

skip taube,
david fenton,
& all the brothers & sisters

too numerous to mention
but my brother took care of us all
& made sure we had a place

to sleep at night,
& food on the table,
& some kind of raggedy car or van

to get around in
& do our work
in the community,

drug help,
ozone house,
the free people's clinic,

the tribal council,
the people's food co-op,
the free concerts

in the parks all summer,
the people's ballroom
& countless benefit concerts,

rainbow trucking company,
energy sound company,
rainbow records & recording,

the *ann arbor sun*,
the live broadcasts on wnrz,
the children's community center,

the ann arbor blues & jazz festival,
the human rights party,
the ann arbor cable commission

where my brother was a commissioner
& ran for city council
in the 2nd ward

& worked & worked
for the good of his community
without thought of personal reward,

my brother david
gave everything he had
for the movement we were part of,

he gave
everything he had
& inspired his comrades

to give as much as they could
for as long as it seemed
that we would still be able

to make a transformation
in the social order
that surrounded us—

to make a better world,
to feed & house & care for
our entire citizenry,

to provide medical services
to people with illnesses
of every sort,

to champion freedom
of the press & public access
to all mass media,

to provide a genuine education
& access to vital information
for each & every person,

to place music & the arts
at the very center
of our educational system,

to support the nation's artists
with life-long stipends
to secure the future of our culture,

to put an end to war,
to completely dismantle
all nuclear weapons,

to empty the penitentiaries
of all the prisoners
of the war on drugs,

to provide jobs and livelihoods
for each & every citizen
for every year of our lives,

to break up the monopolies
of the international corporations
over every aspect of our culture,

to handcuff the bankers
& real estate developers
who have ruined our country,

to elect a black man president
& legalize medical marijuana
in the state of michigan—

this is the kind of world
my brother david believed in
& lived & fought for

to the very end
of what we called the revolution
& then fought on

to clear the books
of the bitter results
of our failures,

then to leave ann arbor
with his wife liz, to settle
in healdsburg, california

to defend himself
against the federal drug charges
triggered by the snitching shure brothers,

& then to live his life
for the next 20 years
as a private citizen

committed to hard labor
with the clearwater construction company
digging up the ground & installing

huge concrete water tanks
at remote homesteads
in the hills of northern california

& conducting his research
into the history of warfare
& writing his brilliant poems

strictly for the pleasure
of expressing himself
through the composition of verse—

ah my brother david
gave up his working life in california
in 1999 & moved with liz

to the florida panhandle
to help liz's mother
care for her husband

in the final throes
of alzheimer's disease
& then settled in

next to a lake
on the outskirts
of the little city of defuniak springs

& partnered with his mother-in-law
in the operation
of her used book store,

surrounded by literature
of every description,
reading his murder mysteries

just like his brother,
going fishing,
writing his poems,

finally fighting his addiction
to alcohol & joining a.a.
& working the steps

with his new-found friends
who carried my brother
through his last 4 years,

proud of his sobriety,
in love with his wife,
& writing his ass off until the end—

oh my baby brother,
my little rootie tootie,
my heart & my right hand,

hero of the revolution,
unacknowledged saint
of the struggle

to create a higher form of life
on this ugly planet
through persistent sacrifice

& ecstatic practice,
doing the work
& taking the punishment

& doing the work
& doing the work
as long as we can

                                        —detroit
                                  october 23 >
                            november 2–3, 2008

#42

"sweet & lovely"

for soul lucille

it's a hell
of a thing, when the woman
you've loved
longer than anything

turns her back on you
& walks away
after 26 years to-
gether, with not so much

as a proper goodbye, a form
of rejection
that cuts so deeply
you don't even know

how to recover
your sense of self
worth, or the confidence
that a woman

will give you her love
& make you the man
she desires
without limitation—oh

the time it takes
for the hurt to recede
& for your feelings
to return,

& then one day
at the hotel utopia
in amsterdam
everything changes

when a beautiful friendship
turns into something deeper
& sweeter, & my heart
starts to swell

& the blood
starts to rush
to the groin again
& my love

comes tumbling down
& it all comes back
like i never thought it would
& suddenly i'm whole,

overcome with emotion
& flush with desire
to get as close to you
as i possibly can,

to be inside you,
to make you feel
as full as i feel
inside my heart

when we're together, soul
to soul, head
over heels & heedless
of the consequences

of where this feeling
will take us, but ready
to go there right now
with you,

my sweet baby,
my lost-found love,
my psychedelic dream girl, oooh
my lovely soul lucille

—genoa
june 19, 2008/
detroit
october 5 > 8, 2008

#43

"bye-ya"

for my daughter sunny
on her 24th birthday

in the middle of my 50th
year on this planet,
each one of them spent
in the great lake state
of michigan, once & future o-
jibwa territory, & my only home
in this world to date—

in this 50th year
it is time
to leave behind
the land of my humble ancestors
& resettle in the southland
of my sunniest dreams, where the weather
better suits our clothes, & the music

fills up the very air,
& the sunshine we seek
may help us mend
our broken hearts, & lend us
the balm of hope
to make this new beginning
in the middle of our life—

so let me say my goodbyes
to harrison & clare,
ubly, kinde & port austin,
owosso, wyandotte, berkley & flint,
davison, albion, beloved detroit,
the house of correction, ann arbor,
jackson & marquette—

& while my darling sunny
& my dear mother elsie
must be left behind, & all the family
of my wife penny's
left in detroit, we're moving out
& heading south
to the land of new orleans—

where the wild indians
& the brass bands, & the social aid
& pleasure clubs
rule the streets, & the ancestral spirits
inhabit the atmosphere
of the city, where we may always reach them
with our prayers—

awww,
c'mon, baby,
it's time for us to go
way down behind the sun,
time to leave all our winters behind
& lift our spirits up
to the southern sky—

bye-ya

—*"edward blackwell tribute"*
riverboat hallelujah, tulane avenue
new orleans
may 4, 1991/
harmonie park, detroit
may 25, 1991/
detroit, august 6, 2003

#44

"monk's dream"

for tyree & karen guyton & sam mackey

in the middle of the night
on the east side of detroit
off behind mack & gratiot,

on heidelberg street
where a lot of old houses
be burnt out

or just falling apart
& big weeds be growing up
where there used to be houses,

on heidelberg street
in the middle of the night
when the moon is high in the sky

& people be asleep in they beds
dreaming of new refrigerators
full of groceries for they babies

& maybe a new car outside,
or a number they can hit tomorrow,
put it in a box,

drag a bunch of boxes out
in the vacant lot across the street
& pile them up on top one another,

paint 'em all different colors,
hang a pink bicycle
up in a tree painted polka dot,

nail some old plastic doll bodies
& maybe some road signs
up on the front porch next door

where the people been gone so long
& stick in a telephone booth,
put a television on the porch roof

& plug it in,
change the channel once or twice,
a toy airplane in a bird cage

on the top of the house,
some plastic legs
sticking out the front window,

all different colors of paint
& objects of every description
stuck or nailed on somehow

all over the abandoned house,
"sometimes a thing
just needs some stripes"

says grandpop, 91, who can see
the things that maybe we can't
in the middle of the night,

like the doll in the attic window,
"she's reaching out for help,"
& the line of doors in the field

on the other side of the street,
they came from houses
that used to be here,

they came from old refrigerators
& wrecked taxicabs, they standing there
cocked every which way

& down on the corner of ellery
they got 3 big old vacant lots,
one got a raggedy boat in it

filled with junked tires,
one got a pile of oil drums
painted up in bright colors,

the other one got more doors
all lined up in a row
like tyree say,

"there are so many openings
in life, you just have to pick
the right ones"—

the music comes up in the background
out of the little speaker
on the radio by the porch, it's thelonious

with charlie rouse, "monk's dream"
& the peoples indoors sleeping
turn over in they beds,

a smile on they faces,
they know in their dreams
it's just tyree & karen & grandpop out there

on heidelberg street
in the middle of the night
turning their neighborhood inside out

—harmonie park
detroit
may 26, 1988/

renumbered
@ genoa
june 19, 2008

#45

"trinkle, tinkle"

for budd johnson

"i mean," budd johnson sez,
"they wasn't calling it
bebop then. even monk
couldn't explain it,

but dizzy could,
& he could develop. but now,
i do remember this about monk.
monk's feelings got hurt

because dizzy & charlie
was getting all of the credit
for this music,
this style—

          "i used to go
over to monk's house with him,
drink some wine with him. 'come on,
i want you to hear

what i'm doing,' he said, 'i'm gonna let them
take that style, & go a-
head, & i'm gonna get
a new style.'

"i used to go
over to monk's
& sit down & drink. his mother
would fix some food for us,

& he would just play for me,
all this funny-type music
that he was playing. & he had gone
altogether different

from what he had been doing. i said,
'hey man . . . .
that's outtasight! what're you doing,
whaddayou call that?'

'i don't know man, it's just . . .
you know?' he couldn't
explain it to me. & i never
thought of monk

as a great piano player, but he
would fumble on that piano
& get these things out
& made all the dissonant

chords,
& major seconds,
& minor seconds. & i said
'hey, man,

that's outtasight.' 'well,
i'm going on now
with my new music,'
he said. & he did.

he did go

     right on along

          with his new

              music."

—*harmonie park, detroit*
july 11, 1988/
detroit
august 6, 2003/
amsterdam
June 4, 2007

reference: dizzy gillespie
with al fraser,
to be, or not . . . to bop
(*doubleday, 1979*), p. 219

"these foolish things"

for penny

i was wrong,
you were wrong,

can't two wrongs
make a right this once

or do we have to cancel
everything?

—*greektown, detroit*
october 2, 1987

#47

"bemsha swing"

for nat hentoff

"i used to have a phobia
about pictures
or anything on a wall
hanging just a little bit

crooked," nellie monk
told nat hentoff. "thelonious
cured me. he nailed a clock
to the wall

at a very slight angle,
just enough
to make me furious.
we argued about it

for 2 hours,
but he wouldn't let me
change it. finally
i got used to it. now

anything can hang
at any angle
& it doesn't bother me
at all."

—harmonie park
detroit
november 25, 1988

"reflections"

for penny

many ladies
there have been
in my life

who have graced me
with their charms
& held me so

sweetly
for so long
as warmth remained

but only three
have shared the burden
of my daily ways—

my first love lasted
13 long years
thru all sorts of hell

until things got better
& then it was over,
my dear first wife & the mother

of my 2 lovely daughters.
my second love i wed
in common law

in 1979, & in '81
& in '82, & again in '84—
4 times around & now

it's the 2 of us to stay.
& my third love lasted
no more than a year

before she threw me out—so
like they say, you win some
& you lose some

& if life is good to you, some
good woman will take you in
& love you as long as she can

—detroit
january 14, 1985/
august 6, 2003

#49

"let's call this"

for jayne cortez

baseball, poetry, &
rhythm & blues—
& all three

in one most
glorious day,
april 15, 1982—

let's call this
opening day,
like the sky

opened up & grinned
all over detroit
& at the shrine

of truth & beauty
at michigan & trumbull
even the tigers came thru

4 to 2
over toronto
& at the detroit

institute of arts
jayne cortez
made the scene

with her crazy
poetry-
making machine

& to top it off,
making his first
detroit appearance

in recorded memory,
the pride
of orange, texas,

ladies &
gentlemen, that mighty
man of music, mister

clarence
"gatemouth"
brown!

so let's call this a
perfect
day then, & please

please, please,
i'm down on my knees
begging for more—

80 more
home games to go, &
let the hits just

keep on coming
day after day
for the rest of the year!

—*detroit*
april 17, 1982

#50

"think of one"

for dar

i searched
my heart
& found you there (actually

there's no question
i was looking
for you there, after all

these years a part
of me is you, is there
any reason why we don't

or can't we
be to-
gether at last, at a

time like this, haven't we
waited
long enough?

—detroit
april 15, 1982

#51

"friday the 13th"

for mike liebler

any day
can be the lucky one,
or the one with your number

written all over it, 123
507 in the poet's case,
walking out

the front door
of the penitentiary,
8:30 p.m.

14 years ago today,
two times 7 years the cycle
of struggle, to make it through

in one piece, on the yard
or in these streets, "anyone
who can pick up a frying pan

owns death," burroughs said,
& sometime in new york city
coming home from the recording studio

walking up to his front door,
john lennon with a gun
stuck in his face,

oh,
oh, sweet giant of song,
with heart of huge dimension

& eyes deep in the sky,
there has to be a day
when each of us must pass

beyond this tedious sphere,
to enter some wondrous place
of which we do not know

whether we're ready or not,
some other place or space
out of time

where no punk with a weapon
will ever press you again
or blow off your face

out of the depths
of his madness, no one
will hold us

against our will
in a cell with bars in front
& back, 6 feet by 4 feet

by 8 feet high,
no one will take us
out of our natural lives

& send us away from here
by means of some murderous fantasy
in which we are denied

everything we have lived for—
oh please let us die
at the end of our own time

& not before, free
in our world of strife,
let us have life

as long as we can
& please, let there be men
like monk & john lennon

to share of their hearts
& light up our ways
as long as we may live

—detroit
friday, december 13/
december 30, 1985

#52

"we see"

for celia

sometimes it happens
just that way,
what burroughs calls "inter-
section points," like

just now, i'm talking
to my mother
on the phone, she wants to know
what happened to that check?

& the 'sons of the blues'
come up on the tape
in the background, singing
"where's my money"

& at my front door,
the kid who's been cutting the lawn
he's there too, waiting
to get paid

—oak park, mi
july 15, 1984

#53

"smoke gets in your eyes"

for penny

when i'm high i think of you
& how you entered my life
on devil's night, 1979,
two days before your birthday—

i fell in love with you
the minute i first saw you
walking across the room
to serve a tray of drinks, cobb's

corner bar, the same year
dear henry was killed, & my heart
has never been the same
since i fell for you—

eight years we were together,
four times we've been apart,
i helped you bring up your children
& you helped me bring up mine—

we would be so high together
in so many ways, blasted on smoke
or cocaine, loving each other
so much it was always fresh

& new again, making love so long
my head floods with pictures
of your sweet cunt in my face,
my dick in your mouth, your ass

pushing up at me or pulsing
around my middle finger, your hands
rubbing your pussy for me
& your titties, or fondling my cock

until nothing else mattered
& all our fights would be forgotten,
all the threats of leaving,
everything would wash away

in a high burst of cum
& perfect sweetness of feeling, sex
so good that we could fuck
even when we weren't speaking to each other,

or your ways would drive me mad
or i would piss you off
with some stupid shit i'd say
or the dreadful crush of poverty

with three or four girls to feed
at any given time, & literally not a dollar
in our collective pocket, behind in the rent
to the point of eviction,

but our friends would keep us high
out of the goodness of their hearts
& our sex life would keep us together
when nothing else was working

or when we'd split up, & try to find
more happiness than we could give each other
in the arms of different lovers
but we'd keep coming back

& keep coming back,
the sound of your voice in my ear
months later when you'd call me
would make my dick get hard

& cancel all my resolve
to make life work without you,
baby, what we had was so deep
& so strong, for so long

i thought we'd always recover
& when you called me on my last birthday
two months after i'd moved out for good
i was so happy to have you back again

i tried to forget why i'd left
but there it was, we got so high after that
i didn't know whether to hold you
or keep letting you go, what was fun for me

was more or less than kicks for you,
not an occasional puff to make sex higher
but running the streets copping cracks
& wolfing them down, too much

was never enough any more
& you could leave me waiting on you
hours or days without a call
while you chased the pipe with lita

or your geeked-up brother
or some other strung-out characters
& then bring them by my place with you
like the morning of your birthday

when you showed up for saturday night
at 7:00 a.m. sunday morning,
the four of you sucked up the last cracks
& when they finally left you with me

you cried in my arms for hours
because all the smoke was gone
& you still wanted more—
you made my heart ache for you then,

baby, you were so pitiful
& i wanted to make you happy
but i didn't have what you wanted—
so everything was up & down

all the way through november, the highs
were so high, but the lows
went lower than ever, like the saturday
after thanksgiving, when you took off work

to help me move my belongings all night
after i was evicted again, & i had to leave
for a gig in chicago in the morning,
but when i drove you home

you wouldn't take me in the bedroom
we had shared for years
& sent me on the road all geeked up
feeling worse than a stranger—

then you stood me up again
when i got back in town
& got all salty with me
when i wanted an explanation—

that was where it ended.
i gave up on you.
i couldn't love you any less,
but i couldn't take any more.

the holidays passed.
i didn't want to see you.
i put you out of my life
& went about my business, i fell in love

with a wonderful friend
who treats me like she cares for me
& makes me happy every day,
every time i see her. we never fight

& we try to accomodate one another
coming from two very disparate places
at diverse rates of speed.
this is good for me. we can talk

about our feelings,
& what's on our minds,
& i don't have to fry my brains
trying to figure out where she's coming from.

so in the middle of all this,
out of nowhere you call me up,
you're coming to see me,
all of a sudden i want you,

i'm excited, i wait all night,
you don't show up. two days later
you call with a story,
you had to go to the hospital,

maybe you'll see me that night
at the doctor john show. so sure enough
there you are, but you're with some chump
you have to stop & introduce me to.

my mind is totally blown.
but what really kills me is,
my nose is wide open, & i'm ready
to fuck up all the happiness in my life

just to suck your pussy again,
& watch you suck my dick. this is sick.
i'm ashamed of myself like a dog,
but there it is. i want you so fucking bad

even though your mind is all twisted up
& there's nothing but pain & confusion
waiting for me inside you, squatting
in your little heart

like fucking satan himself
hunched outside the gates of hell
with a glass dick for a pitchfork
& a brimstone torch. you know i

want your wicked ass,
devil woman, but dig this,
the smoke has left my eyes, & the fire
i burned for you so long

is finally going out, & like they say
when that lovely flame dies
that's the end of it. please,
leave me alone. don't call me. stay the fuck

out of my life. i might still *want* you,
but you don't have what i need,
& this time i'm not settling for any less
than everything i've got coming.

you don't have it,
i don't need you,
it's all over, this is the end
of my motherfucking song, & now i'm gone

—*harmonie park*
detroit
february 2, 1988

#54

"locomotion"

for penny

there's got to be a way
to deal with how i feel
& not just go
off on you again—

i know that i've been wrong
in life so many times,
it was a big
mistake for me to leave you—

now every where i go
i'm looking for your face
in every crowd,
in every car i pass by—

i'm slowly going mad,
i've almost lost my mind,
this life is not
worth while to be without you—

i know so many things
went wrong for you & me
but it was me
who started all our problems—

oh baby take me back,
there's got to be a way,
i love you &
i want you more each day

—*harmonie park*
detroit
june 21/29, 1988

#55

"hackensack"

for mary lou williams

named for the new jersey town
across the river from manhattan,

scenic hackensack,
home of the rudy van gelder studios

where blue note & prestige
did most of their recording,

this tune was recorded as "rifftide"
by coleman hawkins in 1944

when monk was in his 52nd street band,
the changes were from "lady, be good"

but the concept was monk's, & he got it
from an asch records session with hawk

& the great mary lou williams,
its true composer,

born in pittsburgh in 1910,
sweetheart of kansas city jazz in the '30s

with andy kirk & his 12
clouds of joy orchestra,

resident of harlem in the '40s,
an apartment in hamilton terrace

with a good piano
where the composers

& piano players came
to work out their charts,

a close friend of tadd dameron
& dizzy gillespie, mary lou knew bird

as a teenager in k.c.
& again in new york, chicago, harlem,

mary lou williams was a composer
of hundreds of tunes & major works

including "trumpet no end"
for the duke ellington orchestra,

"camel hop" & "roll em" for benny goodman,
"cloudy", "steppin' pretty," "walking

& swinging" & "froggy bottom"
for the twelve clouds of joy, & in 1946

she played her "zodiac suite"
with the new york philharmonic orchestra

in the first symphonic jazz concert
ever to be staged, mary lou williams

spanned the generations
from pre-swing jazz

to cecil taylor, & in the '40s
she was a champion of bebop

among the musicians of her generation:
"we were inseparable," she says, "monk,

bud powell & i. we were always
together,

every day,
for a long time." she also reveals

that many of her pieces
showed up under different names

on the records of other musicians, like
"little joe from chicago" as "blues

in the night," or "what's your story,
morning glory" as "black coffee,"

or "walking & swinging", which appeared
at least 3 times

under other titles, like "opus
caprice" by al haig, "symphony hall swing"

by sonny stitt, & "rhythm-a-ning"
by monk in 1957, by which time

ms. williams had abandoned
entertainment & the performing arts,

worked as a nurse & committed
her music to the church, writing

"mary lou's mass"
& many other original works

in the spiritual idiom.
she reminds us: "jazz

came out of the suffering
of the early black slaves; i think

it was born
in mississippi.

when i was 7 years old,
i used to hide

under my great-grandparents' bed
& hear them talk about that,

how the slaves
created the music

& so forth. all of that music
is spiritual music. it's for human beings,

not for someone to walk around with an ego.
naturally the creators

could play it
with a better feel,

but it was created
for everybody to play."

—ann arbor
christmas
december 25, 1985

#56

"portrait of an eremite"

(*monk alone in paris*)

perhaps a solitary madman
but certainly a genius
of unique proportion

standing out against the environment
like in paris in june
of 1954, or anywhere

he might hang his hat,
in the recording studio
alone with the piano,

fully suited
in the early summer heat
& the awful closeness of the room

while rivulets of sweat
drip from his brow
& beneath his chapeau

& cascade from his chin
onto the keyboard
like a man in a sauna,

but picking out his thoughts
on the slippery keys
of ivory & ebony

with careful deliberation
as if he were sitting instead
on a big block of ice

—detroit
august 29, 2007

"work"

for marc crawford

monk once was busted
along with bud powell
sitting in a car
with a packet of heroin
on the seat between them.

they say the dope
was bud's, but monk
wouldn't say
one way or the other
when the police wanted to know.

"new york's finest"
took new york's finest
pianists to court, & monk's wife nellie
tried to reason with thelonious
from her own understanding:

"every day i would plead with him,"
nellie told marc crawford,
"'thelonious,
get yourself out
of this trouble. you didn't

do anything.' but he'd just say,
'nellie,
i have to walk the streets
when i get out.
i can't talk.'"

monk never said a word
& the judge
popped him in the cooler
for 60 long days & nights,
which wasn't the half of it

because the police
took his cabaret card
(& bud's too), & he couldn't work
in the nightclubs
for 6 more years.

"everybody was saying
thelonious was weird
or locked up,"
nellie remembered, "but
they just talked that way

because they'd never see him.
he hated to be asked
why he wasn't working,
& he didn't want to see anybody
unless he could buy them

a drink at least. besides,
it hurts less
to be passed over for jobs
if you aren't around to hear
the others' names called.

it was a bad time.
he even had to
pay
to get into
birdland."

—harmonie park
detroit
november 25, 1988

reference: marc crawford,
"the sphere of music"
(new musical express, may 21, 1983)

special thanks to david swain

#59

"blue monk"

dirty dozen version

pardon me boy,
pardon me boy,
ain't you gonna
shine my shoes?

i say pardon me boy,
pardon me boy,
when you gonna
shine my shoes?

that's why monk
's blue, wouldn't you-oo
be ba-lue-oo
too?

—oak park, mi
march 20, 1984

#60

"just a gigolo"

for joyce

i'm not quite sure
how to take this, but

for the first time
in my life

i think you want me
just for sex

& not all those other things
we talked about—

i'm not quite sure,
but i think i like it

even better
like this

"i want to be happy"

for orrin keepnews

"one thing,"
says orrin keepnews,
"about making suggestions

to monk:
you need never fear
that he might accept one

he considers second-rate
merely to be polite
or politic"

—detroit
march 16, 1985

reference:
notes to riverside lp-235

#62

"the way you look tonight"

for sonny rollins

"i was trying to finish high school
at the same time as rehearsing
& playing all night," sonny rollins says,
"whenever i was *able* to play.

thelonious had a young band
& he gave me a chance. monk
was a magician. the musicians
would look at his music & say,

'oh no,
this is impossible,
how can i make that jump
from here

to there,
it can't be done,
hey man,
what *is* this?' & by the time

we'd leave that night,
everyone would be playing it
& it would be
beautiful."

—harmonie park
detroit
july 11, 1988

reference: gary giddins,
riding on a blue note,
(*ny: oxford univ press, paper*), *p. 121*

"more than you know"

for miles davis

an english jazz critic
says to miles davis,
"i've just been listening
to that first lp you made

back in 1948 (sic)
& i'd like to tell you
that i think you've improved
all out of recognition

since then." & miles sez,
"when did you first hear that record?"
"about a year ago,"
the critic says back.

"man,"
sez miles davis,
"you should have heard it
in 1948!"

—harmonie park
detroit
may 27, 1988

reference: kenneth tynan
liner notes to
prestige p-24012

#64

"bags groove"

for philip & milton hale

the sound of Detroit
ever pulsates, from before
& even after the end
of world war 2

when the arsenal
of democracy
carved out the freeways
& built up the suburbs

& started moving
the tax base
& all the white people
out—

but the cars
kept rolling
off the assembly lines
& the peoples

all had jobs
& paychecks
& cars & homes
of their own for a while

& the schools
taught music & art
to the children
of the working class

& the pulsation
of the music
grew ever stronger
& more powerful

& the city grew huge
with the artistry
& soulfulness
of its great musicians—

wardell gray,
billy mitchell,
tommy flanagan,
donald byrd,

paul chambers,
doug watkins,
curtis fuller,
pepper adams,

louis hayes,
roy brooks,
alice mcleod,
kenny "pancho" hagood,

betty carter,
barry harris,
ali muhammad,
sir roland hanna,

sonny red,
louis smith,
herbie williams,
wsilbur harden,

abe woodley,
joe brazil,
hugh lawson,
ernie farrow,

art mardigan,
frank isola,
frank morelli,
frank rosolino,

bernard mckinney,
ray mckinney,
earl mckinney,
harold mckinney,

terry pollard,
dorothy ashby,
jimmy wilkins,
milller brisker,

todd rhodes,
maurice king,
thomas "beans" bowles,
donald townes,

lamonte hamilton,
claire rocquemore,
moon mullins,
in & out of the penitentiary,

willie wells,
melvin mccray,
boo boo turner,
willie metcalf,

& in the modern era,
sam sanders,
kenny cox,
wendell harrison,

marcus belgrave,
donald walden,
george bohannon,
bennie maupin,

teddy harris,
charles boles,
bess bonnier,
jack brokensha,

kirk lightsey,
cecil mcbee,
freddie waits,
phil lasley,

ali jackson,
oliver jackson
ron carter,
j.d. allen,

framk gant,
sundiata keita,
sundiata o. mausi,
brian akunda hollis,

mo hollis,
bobby mcdonald,
pierre rochon,
hach gregegian,

lonnie hillyer,
charles mcpherson,
ronnie johnson,
george garnett,

joe henderson,
leon henderson,
ernie rodgers,
marvin "doc" holiday,

bud spangler,
roderick hicks,
george davidson,
ralphe armstrong,

charles moore,
danny spencer,
phil ranelin,
ralph "buzzy" jones,

lyman woodard,
ron english,
larry smith,
leonard king,

allen barnes,
robert lowe,
norma jean bell,
regina carter,

marion hayden,
eileen orr,
gaye lynn mckinney,
jaribu shahid,

reginald "shoo-be-doo" fields,
rodney whitakar,
tani tabbal,
faruq z. bey,

geri allen,
kenny garrett,
james carter,
james "blood" ulmer,

rj spangler,
john "t-bone" paxrton,
james o'donnell,
keith kaminsky—

working their motor city magic
on the ineffable,
on the ineluctable,
on the irrefutable,

on the eternal,
non-stop,
24-hour-a-day groove
laid down by bags

& the men & women
who came after him
out of northwestern high school
& miller

& cass tech
& northern high
& wayne state university
& all over the city,

reaching out from Detroit
to the ends of the earth—
this is the music
that made the motor city great

—jazz loft,
greektown,
detroit
july 30, 2007/

amsterdam espresso
2nd & forest
detroit
august 28, 2007 /

russell street
eastern market
detroit
april 20–21 > osctober 8, 2008/

55 peterboro
cass corridor
detroit
may 10, 2020

#65

"swing spring"

for antoniello "rent"

ah, to close out
the springtime
in italia dolce

& swing
into summer, with the sun a-
blaze

in the roman sky
& the moon on full
in abruzzo,

for il poeta americano
how sweet it is
to be so alive!

—route a-24
roma > fossa cesia
june 30, 2007

#66

"the man i love" (tk 2)

for dr. dorothy

love is
as love does,
my dear, &

what love does
is go with love
together, not a-

part
or in some
other country, but

to live as one
& to be there
at all times

for each other—so
if I could be the
man you love, then

there would be no
question
of your whereabouts

& to drop out
or disappear
would not be

love,
but its opposite
number,

as when monk
refused to comp
for miles—

they may have a-
voided fisticuffs, as rumor
would have had it, but miles

would never again in-
vite monk
to make the date

—*route a-24*
roma > fossa cesia
june 30, 2007

discography

volume one: blue notes

THELONIOUS MONK DISCOGRAPHY
By Michael Cuscuna

Thelonious Monk Sextet, New York City, October 15, 1947

Idrees Suleiman (trumpet); Danny Quebec West (alto saxophone); Billy Smith (tenor saxophone); Thelonious Monk (piano); Gene Ramey (bass); Art Blakey (drums)

BN 308-2	Humphf	Blue Note 560
BN 309-1	Evonce (alternate take)	Mosaic Records
BN 309-4	Evonce (master)	Blue Note 547
BN 310-1	Suburban Eyes (master)	Blue Note 542
BN 310-2	Suburban Eyes (alternate take)	Mosaic Records
BN 311-0	Thelonious	Blue Note 542

Thelonious Monk Trio, New York City, October 24, 1947

Monk (piano); Gene Ramey (bass); Art Blakey (drums)

BN 312-0	Nice Work If You Can Get It (alternate take)	Mosaic Records
BN 312-1	Nice Work If You Can Get It (master)	Blue Note 1575
BN 313-0	Ruby My Dear (alternate take)	Mosaic Records
BN 313-1	Ruby My Dear (master)	Blue Note 549
BN 314-0	Well You Needn't (master)	Blue Note 543
BN 314-1	Well You Needn't (alternate take)	Mosaic Records
BN 315-0	April In Paris (alternate take)	Mosaic Records
BN 315-0	April In Paris (master)	Blue Note 1575

| BN 317-1 | Off Minor | Blue Note 547 |
| BN 316-3 | Introspection | Blue Note LP 1510 |

Note: BN 316 was attempted three times (takes 0. 1. 2) and set aside until after BN 317 was successfully recorded, then completed in the master take.

Thelonious Monk Quintet, New York City, November 21, 1947

George Taitt (trumpet); Sahib Shihab (alto saxophone); Monk (piano); Bob Paige (bass); Art Blakey (drums)

BN 318-3	In Walked Bud	Blue Note 548
BN 319-0	Monk's Mood	Blue Note 1565
BN 320-0	Who Knows (master)	Blue Note 1565
BN 321-1	Round About Midnight	Blue Note 543
BN 320-7	Who Knows (alternate take)	Mosaic Records

Thelonious Monk Quartet, New York City, July 2, 1948

Milt Jackson (vibraharp); Monk (piano); John Simmons (bass); Shadow Wilson (drums); Kenny "Pancho" Hagood (vocals on BN 326 & 327 only)

BN 326-3	All The Things You Are	Blue Note 1201
BN 327-1	I Should Care (alternate take)	Blue Note LA 579-2
BN 327-2	I Should Care (master)	Blue Note 1201
BN 328-0	Evidence	Blue Note 549
BN 329-0	Mysterioso (master)	Blue Note 560
BN 329-1	Mysterioso (alternate take)	Blue Note LP 1509
BN 330-0	Epistrophy	Blue Note 548
BN 331-1	I Mean You	Blue Note 1564

Dizzy Gillespie—Charlie Parker Quintet, New York City, June 6, 1950

Dizzy Gillespie (tp) Charlie Parker (as) Thelonious Monk (p) Curly Russell (b) Buddy Rich (d).

410-4	Bloomdido	Mercury 11058
411-3	An Oscar For Treadwell	Mercury 11082
412-3	Mohawk	Mercury 11082
413-0	My Melancholy Baby	Mercury 11058
414-1	Leap Frog	Mercury 11076
415-1	Relaxin' With Lee	Mercury 11076

Thelonious Monk Quintet with Frankie Passions, New York City, 1951

Idrees Sulieman or Kenny Dorham (tp) Charlie Rouse (ts) Thelonious Monk (p) unknown (b) unknown (d) Frankie Passions (vo). NYC, 1951

| | Especially For You | Spotlite (E) SPJ 135 |
| | Nobody Knows | – |

Thelonious Monk Quintet, New York City, July 23, 1951

Sahib Shihab (as -1/6) Milt Jackson (vib -1/6,9) Thelonious Monk (p) Al McKibbon (b) Art Blakey (d). WOR Studios, NYC, July 23, 1951

BN 392-1	Four In One	Blue Note 1589
BN 393-0	Criss Cross	Blue Note 1590
BN 394-0	Eronel	Blue Note 1590
BN 395-0	Straight, No Chaser	Blue Note 1589
BN 396-0	Ask Me Now (alt. take)	Mosaic MR 4-101
BN 396-1	Ask Me Now	Blue Note 1591
BN 397-0	Willow Weep For Me	Blue Note 1591

Thelonious Monk Sextet, New York City, May 30, 1952

Kenny Dorham (tp -1/8) Lou Donaldson (as -1/8) Lucky Thompson (ts -1/8) Thelonious Monk (p) Nelson Boyd (b) Max Roach (d). WOR Studios, NYC, May 30, 1952

BN 434-1 tk.2	Skippy	Blue Note 1602
BN 435-1 tk.5	Hornin' In (alt. take)	Mosaic MR 4-101
BN 435-3 tk.7	Hornin' In	Blue Note 1603
BN 436-0 tk.8	Sixteen	Mosaic MR 4-101
BN 436-1 tk.9	Sixteen (alt. take)	Mosaic MR 4-101
BN 437-0 tk.10	Carolina Moon	Blue Note 1603
BN 438-0 tk.11	Let's Cool One	Blue Note 1602
BN 439-0 tk.12	I'll Follow You	Mosaic MR 4-101

volume two: prestige

Thelonious Monk Trio

Thelonious Monk (p) Gerry Mapp (b) Art Blakey (d). NYC, October 15, 1952

367	Little Rootie Tootie	Prestige 850
368	Sweet And Lovely	Prestige 795
369	Bye-Ya	Prestige 795
370	Monk's Dream	Prestige 850

Thelonious Monk Trio

Thelonious Monk (p) Gerry Mapp (b) Max Roach (d). NYC, December 18, 1952

399	Trinkle, Tinkle	Prestige 838
400	These Foolish Things	–
401	Bemsha Swing	Prestige PRLP 142
402	Reflections	–

Thelonious Monk Quintet

Julius Watkins (frh) Sonny Rollins (ts) Thelonious Monk (p) Percy Heath (b) Willie Jones (d). NYC, November 13, 1953

531	Let's Call This	Prestige PREP 1352
532-1	Think Of One (alt. take)	Prestige PRLP 7053
532-2	Think Of One	Prestige PREP 1352
533	Friday The Thirteenth	Prestige PRLP 166

Thelonious Monk Quintet

Ray Copeland (tp) Frank Foster (ts) Thelonious Monk (p) Curly Russell (b) Art Blakey (d). Rudy Van Gelder Studio, Hackensack, NJ, May 11, 1954

570	Wee See	Prestige PRLP 180
571	Smoke Gets In Your Eyes	–
572	Locomotive	–
573	Hackensack	–

Thelonious Monk Solo

Thelonious Monk (p). NYC, June 7, 1954

	We See	Vogue (F) 500 104
	Smoke Gets In Your Eyes	–
	Reflections	–
	Off Minor	–
	Eronel	–
	'Round About Midnight	–
	Evidence	–
	Well, You Needn't	–
	Hackensack	–

Thelonious Monk Trio

Thelonious Monk (p) Percy Heath (b -1/3) Art Blakey (d -1/3). Rudy Van Gelder Studio, Hackensack, NJ, September 22, 1954

619	Work	Prestige PRLP 189
620	Nutty	–
621	Blue Monk	Prestige 45-162
622	Just A Gigolo	Prestige PRLP 189

Thelonious Monk—Sonny Rollins Quartet

Sonny Rollins (ts) Thelonious Monk (p) Tommy Potter (b) Art Taylor (d). Rudy Van Gelder Studio, Hackensack, NJ, October 25, 1954

630	I Want To Be Happy	Prestige PRLP 190
631	The Way You Look Tonight	Prestige PRLP 190
632	More Than You Know	Prestige PRLP 190

Miles Davis Quintet

Miles Davis (tp) Milt Jackson (vib) Thelonious Monk (p) Percy Heath (b) Kenny Clarke (d). Rudy Van Gelder Studio, Hackensack, NJ, December 24, 1954

676-1	Bags' Groove	Prestige PRLP 196
676-2	Bags' Groove (alt. take)	Prestige PRLP 7109
677	Bemsha Swing	Prestige PRLP 200
678	Swing Spring	Prestige PRLP 196
679-1	The Man I Love	Prestige PRLP 200
679-2	The Man I Love (alt. take)	Prestige PRLP 7150

Master takes indicate original issue. Only the original issues (generally as 78 rpm singles) are listed above. Alternate takes listed as "Mosaic Records" were first released on *The Complete Blue Note Recordings of Thelonious Monk* by Mosaic Records in 1983, which also contains the complete Thelonious Monk Blue Note discography.

#21–40 *blue notes* information added @ Amsterdam, November 22, 2008

#41–66 *prestige* discography added @ Amsterdam, November 22, 2008